Everything I Know about Life, I Learned from My Dog

Everything I Know about Life, I Learned from My Dog

KRISTIN ANN JONES

gatekeeper press™
Columbus, Ohio

Everything I Know About Life, I Learned From My Dog

Published by Gatekeeper Press
2167 Stringtown Rd, Suite 109
Columbus, OH 43123-2989
www.GatekeeperPress.com

The cover design, interior formatting, typesetting, and editorial work for this book are entirely the product of the author. Gatekeeper Press did not participate in and is not responsible for any aspect of these elements.

Library of Congress Control Number: 2021950644

ISBN (paperback): 9781662923210
eISBN: 9781662923227

For Sarah-
You bring joy to my life. Thank you for
your wisdom, your strength, and your heart.
Keep flying.

U,

Mom

ACKNOWLEDGMENTS

A big dog thank you to the following for all of your pawsitive support in the making of this tail wagging book; Sarah Jones, Steve Jones, the Johanson family, Lacey Jones, Debbie Bates, Diane Walck, Connie Hanly-Skinner, Patti Tauscher-Salladay, the Andrews family, Dawn Clausen, Darlene Miller, and Ann Marie Bahantka. And of course to Archer, if not for him, this book would not come, sit, and stay.

And a top dog thanks to the following dogs and their owners for letting me illustrate them for this dog gone unleashed book.

Page 12 - Archie and Eden Patterson
@assistance.archie

Page 16 - Burton and Emily Keene
@burton_thebendberner

Page 46 - Rya
@ryzewithourpack

Page 60 - Kiki and photographer Steve Watson
@thepieddogwalker

Page 85 - Cooper Cumberdale and Justin Garraux
@cooperthetripod

Page 92 - Chip and Lacey Jones

Page 119 - Harley and Hannah Hickam
@wildwiththem

TABLE OF CONTENTS

The Pack

Home is where the dog is.

Everyday routines can be
adventurous.

To be a pack leader, you need to
earn trust and respect from the
rest of the pack.

Quality time requires everyone's full attention.

Begin each day with a bowl of
tasty food and a hearty walk.

A big welcome is always a treat,
especially at the end of a long day.

Silly moments can become
treasured memories.

Big, sweet eyes are sometimes
a disguise for mischief.

Snuggling is as important as
eating, it's a treat for the heart.

Sometimes we all need
to growl a bit.

It's better to bark than to bite.

Every dog needs to run
off leash at some point.

**Don't jump on someone unless
they give you permission.**

Sharing makes almost
everything better.

Find someone who makes you
want to wag everyday.

When you love someone, try to
love them just the way they are.

**True love is being able to
give and take.**

**Even though we don't live in
dog years, life is still too short.**

The classics never get old.

Everyone drools at a certain point.

**Don't change who you
are, just what you do.**

It isn't hard to teach an old dog
new tricks, it just takes longer.

Healthy Dog

Be confident in your own fur.

You deserve a high five.

Naps are essential, not optional.

Good grooming isn't
showing off; it's healthy.

It's okay to howl when
you need help.

You can still be cute even
if you snore.

**Nothing brings a family
together like good food.**

Sometimes it's good to chew
on something awhile.

Drink more water.

Sleeping upside down can
make your day right side up.

**Sometimes it's better to
make your own trail.**

When your hackles go up,
there is usually a good reason.

Sometimes it's just best
to dive right in.

When it rains, shake it off.

**It's hard to be patient,
but we can all learn.**

**Let others know it's not okay
when they try to jump on you.**

Obstacles are meant for jumping over.

**It's easier to go forward
than backward.**

Toys don't need to be expensive.

Yoga positions like downward
dog can lift you up.

Training
and
Service

**Chasing your tail will
make you dizzy.**

Good instincts jump into action.

Always keep your eye on the ball.

Don't hold grudges, start each day anew.

We can always get stuck when
there is a communication problem.

Always praise the pawsitive.

**Stand firm when you are being
pulled in the wrong direction.**

When one doggie door closes,
another one always opens.

**Try to see when you are
barking up the wrong tree.**

There's no such thing as 'too happy'.

Speak up when it matters most.

Sit awhile and listen to your friends.

Roll over a new leaf and try again.

If something isn't working in
your life, drop it.

Lay down and sleep well.

**Every pilot needs a
good co-pilot.**

A lifelong friend can be
made in a single day.

It's good to have someone
guide you.

Little dogs can do big things.

We can all change the
world with what we do.

Empathy energizes the soul.

A strong bond can't be broken.

Have the courage to go where others don't.

Dog Sense

When a dog howls, she is
singing from the heart.

**Run your day, don't let
it run you.**

Every time a dog smiles, a human smiles back.

Be unbewoofable.

Happiness can be found
anywhere, even a mud puddle.

No matter what you say, a
dog will always listen.

Rescue a dog, they always
rescue you back.

It doesn't matter how big your
ears or spots are, just your heart.

You deserve to be loved the
way your dogs love you.

**Faithful friends will run to you
while others run away.**

You can dig yourself out
of almost anything.

Every season of life brings
wonderful changes.

Trust and follow your instincts.

When life gets messy, clean off
your paws and keep going.

Play like there's no tomorrow.

You are enough, just the way you are.

Whenever you see someone you love,
always wag and be happy to see them.

**Underneath our fur, we
are all the same.**

Hugs are golden.

Nothing compares to knowing someone is thinking of you.

🐾🐾🐾🐾🐾

Playtime

We can all get along, even if we
speak different languages.

**Paying attention means
having both ears up.**

Look for friends who dig you
and like to do the same things.

Everything is easier with friends.

**Doing nothing is actually
doing something for your soul.**

**Everyday is a good day to go
to the park.**

Some of life's best surprises can
be found while taking walks.

You can't stop the wind, but
you can certainly enjoy it.

**You don't have to win
to be a winner.**

Motivation drives with no boundaries.

Wag it since you've still got it.

**If you don't fit in, try
sticking out.**

A wagging tail is
contagious.

Do whatever wags your tail.

**Meandering is a valid
way to get somewhere.**

**Don't be above begging,
sometimes it works.**

If you chase two squirrels at the same time, you might come up empty pawed.

**The grass is always greener
on the side you don't pee on.**

Best friends will embrace your differences and enjoy your similarities.

**Put your paws in the air and
dance like you just don't care.**

Milton Keynes UK
Ingram Content Group UK Ltd.
UKHW051825280823
427634UK00005B/63